T0150366

THE PHILOSOPHY OF
BEER

THE PHILOSOPHY OF
BEER

JANE PEYTON

First published 2021 by
The British Library
96 Euston Road
London NW1 2DB

ISBN 978 0 7123 5347 2
eISBN 978 0 7123 6727 1
Cataloguing in Publication Data
A catalogue record for this book is available
from the British Library

Designed and typeset by Sandra Friesen
Printed and bound in Malta by Gutenberg Press

CONTENTS

INTRODUCTION

IMAGINE IF there was a mystical potion with the power to unite the public, regardless of language, race, religion, politics and social standing. Whoever possessed it would have unassailable authority. This is no fantasy, because the superpower already exists. It is called beer.

Beer is an egalitarian and democratic refreshment that knows no borders. Beer is part of the human condition, and without it life would be diminished. That is the way it has been for thousands of years, ever since persons unknown, in who knows where, first sampled fermented cereal sugars and saw stars.

What is beer? *The Oxford English Dictionary* defines it as:

'An alcoholic liquor obtained by the fermentation of malt.'

The etymology is from Old English *beor*, meaning 'strong drink', which may stem from the Latin verb *bibere*, 'to drink'. Beer is an umbrella term covering multitudinous

1

styles such as Mild, Wheat Beer, Pale Ale, Pilsner and Lambic. They are all beers, just different versions and combinations of four ingredients: water, malted cereal, hops and yeast. Beer is the most widely produced alcoholic beverage in the world, brewed in almost all countries where alcohol is legal, and is the third most consumed drink after water and tea. In several nations, including Germany, Belgium, Czech Republic and England, it is the official drink and unofficial national symbol. Male politicians often use beer to burnish their 'man of the people' credentials, posing full glass in hand and sending a subliminal message that they understand the lives and concerns of the electorate. It may sometimes be an act, but it is effective, and recognises the elemental position beer has in society. Beer is also a tool

ALE OR BEER?

I use the terms 'ale' and 'beer' interchangeably throughout the book, apart from when referring to the medieval era, when there was a distinct difference between the two. During this period, hopped beer and unhopped ale were two separate drinks.

of international diplomacy: President Obama and Prime Minister David Cameron swapped bottles of their local brews during an official visit of the British PM to the White House in 2010, and British leaders have been known to take visiting heads of state to the boozer for the all-important photograph at the bar as they enjoy a pint. When overseas politicians visit the Republic of Ireland it is almost obligatory to get a photo of them holding a Guinness.

Beer is a vast subject, so instead of attempting to cover the entire story in a hundred pages, I have chosen themes that are useful for becoming a pocket Mastermind in Beer Knowledge (styles, food-matching, health benefits and so on). There are historical references throughout, connecting the modern beer drinker with our ancestors, and you will learn much about the drink's significance in our cultural and social evolution.

Apart from tasting delicious, beer makes us jovial. The soundscape of a pub offers an aural clue to support this statement. There is a particular quality to the buzz of conversation between happy drinkers. It is the sound of companionship and unity. The ancient Egyptians had an array of beer styles, and one of them was known as 'Joy Bringer'. Those two words symbolise the essence of beer.

THE SPECIAL RELATIONSHIP

Each year at the beginning of August, London hosts the Great British Beer Festival, the largest celebration of unfiltered and unpasteurised ale on the planet. Thousands of individuals from the UK and overseas congregate for several days of liquid feasting, brought together by the world's favourite alcoholic drink. It is a diverse crowd, and attendees have little in common, but together they create an atmosphere of euphoria, harmony and geniality. The hubbub is indescribable, a merry cacophony punctuated periodically by a big cheer when someone drops a glass and it smashes to the floor. That is as violent as it gets, and happiness prevails because they are all 'here for the beer'.

Just like their beer-crazy opposite numbers thousands of years ago in the Middle Eastern lands of Sumer, Babylon and Egypt, the festival-goers are motivated by the desire for a jollification, to drink and have a good time. Unlike their ancient counterparts, they are not visibly worshipping the deities of beer in ecstatic uninhibited public revels lasting for days, but the sentiment is the same.

'It's just beer' is a phrase no one who drinks it would ever utter. It really isn't just beer, but don't take my word for it: beer has 2,290,000,000 mentions on Google and is indispensable for countless people not just because of the fellowship that comes from having a drink with friends, but because it keeps pubs open, generates tourism, provides employment and contributes taxes to governments. All beer drinkers have millions of unknown friends, and if they met, there would be plenty to talk about because beer is the beverage that launches a thousand conversations.

How can something so ubiquitous and 'everyday' be so momentous to human history? It is impossible to overestimate the significance of beer because it has been, and still is for some, necessary to life – serving as nourishment (liquid bread), refreshment, medicine, a sacred libation for communing with ancestors and divinities, a panacea, a commodity for trading, a way to proffer hospitality, a uniting force and friendship builder, and the way to start a party. Life is beautiful through the lenses of beer goggles.

Right from the beginning beer was beneficial in a physical sense. It is made from dried cereal, which can be stored, so brewing could happen even when sustenance was scarce, thereby providing a crucial supply of regular calories.

So far, so serious. Beer needed something more compelling than just being nutritious. Broccoli is nutritious but it has not had the impact beer has. Why beer and not broccoli? One word: intoxication. Beer is intoxicating, and according to Dr Ronald Siegel, an American psychopharmacologist, this encourages imagination, creativity, extroversion and the affirmative rather than the negative. The alcohol in beer spurs the release of dopamine in the reward centre of the brain where humans experience pleasure. Dr Siegel theorised that we have an innate impulse to seek mind-altering states, whether through alcohol, drugs, psychotropic plants, dancing, love or caffeine, and he called the urge the 'fourth drive', as fundamental as food, drink and sex. A non-academic observation to support the theory is to tally the variety of descriptive expressions for the condition of being drunk – trollied, ganted, loaded, leathered, pickled, snobbled, spangled, banjaxed and wellied are nine of hundreds. Just invent a nonsense term then add 'ed' to the end of it, and in the context of drink being taken it is easy to understand what is meant.

In the Fertile Crescent (modern-day Iraq, western Iran, Jordan, Syria, Israel, Palestine and southeastern Turkey) nomadic hunter-gatherers decided to settle in one place and tend to the crops they had planted. Agriculture is believed to have originated there at least 12,000 years ago. Among the first plants to be domesticated were barley and wheat, to the present day the two main cereals used in brewing. The region is known as the 'Cradle of Civilisation', where the concepts of society, culture, commerce, education, law, bureaucracy and religion developed in settlements built by the former nomads. Did the desire for beer change the habits of humans so profoundly? Anthropologist Dr Solomon Katz of the University of Pennsylvania believes a stable supply of grain was the motivation. Most fans of beer would probably concur, proudly acknowledging that their chosen bevvy can claim such influence.

Alcohol and religion have been associated for millennia. Today, beer still has a divine connection with Roman

ST PANCRAS STATION
BEER LARDER

Eurostar travellers leaving from London St Pancras station may be unaware that the departures area, known as the undercroft, was formerly a giant warehouse constructed specifically to store and distribute beer. The architect used the length of a beer barrel as the unit of measurement for the floor layout. When the station, built for Midland Railway, opened in 1868 it provided brewers in Burton-on-Trent with direct access to the capital so their beer (mostly Pale Ale) could be delivered in hours, rather than several days for canal transportation.

Catholic Trappist monasteries in Europe and the USA, where brewing is overseen by monks. In the creation myths of several civilisations of antiquity, beer was a gift from female goddesses such as Ninkasi (Sumer) for the contentment of humans. For Egyptians, beer came from Sun God Ra, so naturally his daughter Hathor was its goddess. She was known as 'The Lady of Drunkenness' and also represented pleasure, joy, laughter, singing and dancing. In Sumer and Egypt liberal amounts of beer were ceremoniously consumed at public gatherings to honour their deities. Beer contained godly essence and it was mandatory to become intoxicated. There was no shame in being visibly sloshed.

Until societies had an endless supply of clean tap water, beer was a lifesaver. It was a safe method of consuming water, as the alcohol it contains kills pathogens. It was imperative to life and, throughout history, laws were introduced to ensure its purity, protect grain supplies and maintain affordable prices. Magna Carta, arguably the most important legal document in English history, was sealed in 1215 and Clause 35 outlines permitted measures for ale: 'Let there be throughout our kingdom a single measure for wine and a single measure for ale and a single measure for corn, namely "the London quarter".' At the time of Magna Carta, and for centuries afterwards, corn was a generic term used for all cereals. This clause not only gave legal protection to ale but also to the grain that made it.

CLEOPATRA, QUEEN OF THE NILE

Beer drinkers might agree with the Queen of the Nile's quotation when she opined in Shakespeare's *Antony and Cleopatra*, 'My salad days, when I was green in judgement, cold in blood', for she was the first documented person to levy tax on beer and would have needed a cool head indeed to risk something so unpopular in Egypt, a land where life and beer were inseparable.

Beer has been a cash cow for governments ever since; a foolproof source of income, often to fund wars – as was the case with the USA, when beer taxation was initiated to subsidise the efforts of the Federal Army in the Civil War. Successive British governments have taxed individual ingredients, the amount of alcohol and/or the beer itself, and imposed licensing fees. Today Britain's beer tax is among the highest in the world.

What about how beer makes people feel? That initial mouthful, that exhalation of pleasure and the 'ooh, so good' comment – that connection beer has with good times. When consumed in company, especially with friends, something magical happens: contentment, conviviality and wanting to hold on to the mood forever. Humans are social creatures, and beer is the ultimate social drink.

FROM THERE TO EVERYWHERE

EVERY MOUTHFUL of beer is a liquid time machine connecting us through millennia to the person who originally brewed it. And who was the genius that brought enjoyment to so many and spawned a multibillion-pound global industry? No one knows.

Cereals are members of the grass family and include barley, wheat, rice, corn, sorghum, millet, rye and oats. They are dietary staples, and are also used for brewing beer. Analysis of the archaeological remains of sorghum on plant grinders found in a cave in Mozambique reveals that *Homo sapiens* were eating wild cereals at least 100,000 years ago. There is no evidence that Stone Age Mozambiquans turned them into beer, but humans have had access to alcohol ever since the species evolved in Africa around 315,000 years ago. Fruit-bearing trees had existed for millions of years, and ripe fruit ferments in warm temperatures and turns to alcohol. The heady buzz would have enticed humans to create purposely made alcoholic drinks – wine from fruit, mead from honey. When it was discovered thousands of

years later that ground cereals added to water produced beer, life was never the same again.

It is not clear how our predecessors made the discovery but it is doubtful beer was invented; rather it might have been experimentation with germinated grains, where something drinkable developed over time. The process of germination converts starch in the seeds to sugars, which are spontaneously fermented by yeast spores in the air and turned into alcohol. Yeasts are microscopic single-celled biotas classified in the kingdom of fungi. Before cereals were domesticated (*circa* 12,000 BCE) grain was hard to digest by eating, but not if it was soluble in beer. Cereals grew in many regions of the world and because humans are inquisitive, they noticed independently that a nourishing and intoxicating fluid foodstuff could be created from the local species of grain. They may have baked the germinated grains into biscuits or bread cakes and then soaked them in warm water to form a gruel or porridge-type concoction, which automatically fermented to an alcohol level of little more than 5 per cent. At present the earliest archaeological proof of what can be described as beer was uncovered in a cave near Haifa in modern-day Israel. It dates back to 13,000 BCE and was in the form of barley/wheat residue on a stone implement that has been interpreted as a multi-purpose vessel for preparing food and beer. Researchers may find even older remains in future and that is why there is no definitive answer to where and when beer was first brewed.

Good news travels, and beer was good news. Knowledge of the special libation spread by word-of-mouth, trade, conquest and population movement. The Sumerians of what is now southern Iraq developed the first system of writing, *circa* 3300 BCE, in a format known as cuneiform, which consisted of pictographs etched into clay tablets. Some of these provided documentary evidence of beer's cultural importance. A tablet that outlined the daily beer rations for manual labourers is now part of the British Museum's collection of Mesopotamian treasures.

To Sumerians a human was not civilised unless they drank beer, and this was emphasised in the poem *Epic of Gilgamesh*, the world's oldest surviving work of literature composed *circa* 2000 BCE, when the wild man Enkidu was tamed after he consumed beer. Beer was sacred; so sacred that Ninkasi, the goddess of creation, fertility and brewing, was worshipped by ritual imbibing. Her human priestesses were responsible for brewing beer in the temples so her disciples could venerate their deity. The name Ninkasi translates as 'the lady who fills the mouth', and a common greeting was 'May Ninkasi live with you, let her pour your beer everlasting.' A fragment of lyrics to a song reveal the delight Sumerians had in beer:

'As I spin around the lake of beer, while feeling wonderful, feeling wonderful, while drinking beer, in a blissful mood, while drinking alcohol and feeling exhilarated, with joy in the heart and a contented liver – my heart is a heart filled with joy!'

Sumer beer traditions were adopted by the Babylonians who had conquered the region. Brewing beer was so vital it was commercialised, and the growing of grain and permitted beer styles were codified in law by King Hammurabi *circa* 1754 BCE. But while beer was the drink for all, one segment of the population was expected to imbibe beyond the gaze of the public. They were the priestesses, who risked being executed if they entered a tavern for a drink.

Egyptians were inspired by the Sumerian devotion to beer and they embraced it wholeheartedly. Barley and emmer wheat grew in the fertile soils of the Nile valley; by the early Dynastic period (3100–2686 BCE) beer was central to life, and everyone drank it regardless of status. Extensive written and pictorial references reveal the magnitude of beer for the living and the dead. It was a constant right from the start of life, when it was used to anoint newborns, for sustenance, medicine, wages, currency, tax, celebrations and worship. It was even offered as a refreshment in the afterlife, placed inside the tombs of the deceased. Modern beer drinkers often wear T-shirts adorned with messages such as 'Wish you were beer', but slogans are nothing new: an inscription at the Dendera Temple complex reads 'The mouth of a perfectly contented man is filled with beer.'

Egypt's location, bisected by a mighty river and with access to the Mediterranean, facilitated the export of goods including beer to nearby Phoenicia, a nation of seafaring turbo-charged traders situated on the coast of what is now Syria, Lebanon, Palestine and northern Israel. This

helped to broaden the habit of beer drinking. While the neighbours may have been impressed by beer, the Greeks under Alexander the Great, who occupied Egypt from the fourth century BCE, were not. The Hellenes associated it with losers, such as the vanquished Egyptians. Later, when the Romans took power, historian Diodorus Siculus was more complimentary when he wrote in his book *Biblioteca Historica* (first century BCE) about Egyptian beer: '... for smell and sweetness of taste it is not much inferior to wine.'

Cereals have been grown in Europe for more than 8,000 years and, according to archaeological evidence from caves near Barcelona, beer has been brewed there since at least 5100 BCE. When the Romans expanded their realm north and westwards into Hispania, Gaul and Germania (western Europe) from the second century BCE, they observed that the local residents binged on beer, and one commentator wrote of them as turning into 'wild men' when they drank it. With the end of Roman rule in Europe *circa* 476 CE the Catholic Church flourished by establishing monasteries across the continent. In northern countries where grapes did not grow but grain did, one reason for the Church's success was a willingness to adopt some of the local pagan practices, including drinking beer. Breweries were built so monks could make beer for their own consumption, to refresh travellers on pilgrimages, and to raise funds for religious work. This contributed to the eventual masculinisation of brewing in Europe, although for several centuries women continued to be the primary brewers. They were known as alewives and made beer at home on a small scale to supply the family, selling any surplus to neighbours who did not brew themselves.

During the medieval era a revolution happened in Europe that changed brewing for ever – it was the application of hops. So far in this book, 'beer' has been used to describe a drink of fermented cereals, whether it contained hops or not. During the Middle Ages, however, there was a difference between ale and beer. The latter included hops, the former did not, and in Britain the distinction continued as

late as the eighteenth century, when ale too was eventually brewed with hops and the terms ale and beer became interchangeable. Hops were revolutionary because the oily resin in their flowers contains antibacterial compounds that act as a preservative, so beer lasted weeks, unlike unhopped ale, which soured quickly. Extended shelf-life meant that beer could travel further distances without going off and that bulk storage was possible, but it was bad news for alewives; it heralded the beginning of the end for their domestic brewing as beer started to be made in commercial breweries and transported to where demand dictated. In the late fourteenth century, Hamburg in Germany was the largest brewing centre, with hundreds of breweries exporting ale, and later beer, by land and sea via merchants of the Hanseatic League to towns and cities throughout the Baltic, northern Europe and beyond. Little by little, customers accepted the bitter flavour imbued by hops, and brewers appreciated the economic benefits they bestowed.

International exploration, commerce, colonisation and immigration continued to proliferate the desire for beer. In the seventeenth century the Dutch East India Company was a superpower in business, enriched by lucrative trade deals with numerous countries. Beer was introduced into the Land of the Rising Sun when a trading post with a beer hall for company employees was built in Nagasaki. Beer is now Japan's premier drink, and in the twenty-first century Asahi, Kirin and Sapporo – three giant Japanese corporations – own craft breweries in Australia, Britain, Canada, Czech Republic, New Zealand and the USA.

In America, settlers at Jamestown Colony had to endure several thirsty years after arriving in 1607 and quickly exhausting the beer they had brought with them. Supplies from the Mother Country were intermittent, so drinking beer was only a daily activity in their dreams until breweries were built in the 1620s.

Beer refreshed and powered all aspects of human life at work and play during this time. In Britain, as consumption increased due to population growth and a workforce with disposable income, brewers responded by building ever-larger breweries and installing technology for more efficiency. The Industrial Revolution begat hellish, sweat-inducing workplaces such as foundries, so workers were required to drink gallons of beer to rehydrate. Porter, a dark and malty beer, was the libation of choice and made in such vast quantities that vats containing several million pints were a common sight in colossal urban breweries, particularly in London, the pre-eminent brewing city on Earth in the eighteenth and nineteenth centuries.

British ships played a role in introducing beer to regions with no breweries, especially during the years of empire building when Britain's colonial settlements covered great swathes of the planet. From the mid-eighteenth century, beer brewed near London's East India Dock, and later in Burton-upon-Trent, slaked the thirst of traders and colonists with what came to be known as India Pale Ale. Meanwhile, Porter was the initial beer consumed in Australia, carried with the First Fleet sent to establish the penal colony in Botany Bay in 1788.

German immigrants were influential in establishing pale lager as the planet's most popular style after they established breweries in Argentina, Brazil, Chile, China, Namibia and, most notably, the United States of America. Two of the US companies founded in the nineteenth century are still in business – Yuengling and Coors (now Molson-Coors). It was a German hired by a small Dutch

brewery in Amsterdam who in the 1880s devised the beer which built the fortune and reputation of Heineken. The company went on to expand globally, especially in Africa and the Far East, by introducing brewing into countries with no local beer industry.

What would the early brewers think of our beer? Even if they did not realise it was the evolution of their own fermented cereal, they would be familiar with the happiness it bestows, and that is a powerful reason for beer's global reach and its enduring popularity.

CHEERS!

Beer still inspires people to sing together, and in the twenty-first century drinkers also have an anthem called 'Cheers to Beer', written by this author and composed by Catherine Houghton with these lines and others:

'What drink elates us and exhilarates us, let's
    raise a glass of beer.
Nature's gift, water, hops, malt and yeast, a
    wholesome panacea,
And the whole world unites with their
    favourite pint, let's raise a glass of beer.'

The anthem was written for people to sing on Beer Day Britain, the UK's national beer day, held annually on 15 June – the same date Magna Carta was sealed in 1215.

SOMETHING'S BREWING

Naturalis Historia, written by Roman philosopher Pliny the Elder in the first century CE, was the model for later encyclopaedias. As the name suggests, it covered a plethora of natural subjects, including alcohol, and Pliny celebrated wine and European beer, about which he wrote, 'The nations of the west also have their own intoxicant, made from grain soaked in water.'

It is true that beer is composed of up to 95 per cent water, and that mouthfeel, flavour and body are affected by its mineral-salt content. Modern-day brewers can alter the composition of the water by adding or subtracting minerals, but before they were able to do that the local water influenced the style of beer. In Britain's West Midlands, where the medium-hard water with calcium chloride is good for sweeter beers, Mild and Brown Ale were popular. Very hard water, high in calcium bicarbonate, efficiently extracts colour from malt and is found in the Dublin area, where dark Stout is the main beer. Plzeň (anglicised as Pilsen) in the Czech Republic has ultra-soft water for perfect Pilsner lager.

Brewers take three ingredients – water, cereal and hops – then brew them together, add yeast, and a few days later the result is beer. That suggests brewing is simple, and on paper it is, but in practice it is not easy to produce good beer. All alcoholic drinks start with a source of sugar, which is fermented and converted to alcohol. In the case of beer, it derives from cereal, usually barley, but depending on style or recipe, wheat, oats, rye, rice or corn are added too. In certain African countries where traditional rural home-brewing is practised, locally grown millet or sorghum are employed, as they have been for thousands of years.

Like their Sumerian and Egyptian forebears did, most brewers today use malted cereal. Malting entails germinating and kilning the grains. Depending on the kiln temperature the germinated malt will be gently toasted, roasted or charred, altering the colour and flavour, which in turn impacts on the beer hue and how it tastes. Malts are selected according to the style of beer to be brewed, then ground into a rough powder known as grist and placed in a vat called a mash tun. Hot water filters through it, collecting sugar, colour and flavour to form a sugary fluid called wort. Eventual alcohol strength is determined by the amount of fermentable sugars it contains. The next stage is to transfer the wort into a brewing kettle and boil it with hops. Hops are used for flavour, aroma and bitterness, and because they preserve the beer. When the boil is complete, the brew is cooled and sent to a fermenting tank. Cultured yeast is added or, if the brewer prefers spontaneous fermentation, they wait for airborne yeast spores to land on the brew and start the maelstrom known as fermentation. Individual yeast cells consume the sugars, and the by-products are alcohol, carbon dioxide and, depending on the strain of yeast, hundreds of aroma and flavour compounds. After fermentation is complete, the beer is matured in a conditioning tank for days or weeks to develop complexity in readiness for packaging.

Nowadays brewing combines art and science and there are specific vessels for each stage, as well as gadgets and technology to finesse it. Today's brewer looking back at their ancestral counterpart would recognise their intentions but little else about the process. Women were the original brewers, because beer is food and food preparation was their domain. Although commercial brewing is now dominated by men, in some parts of Africa and the Amazon beer is still made communally for villagers by women. The sacred beer of indigenous Central and South American tribes is called *chicha*, and some of it is still created the way it always has been by women hand-grinding maize, dampening the flour and forming it into small balls. One at a time these are placed in the mouth and rolled around the tongue until saturated in saliva. This activates the enzyme ptyalin, thereby sweetening the corn starch and releasing fermentable sugars. The cereal balls are dried in the sun, then stirred in hot water for an hour. As it cools, the mixture separates

into three layers: liquid on the top, a jelly-like material in the middle, and grains on the bottom. The middle layer is cooked and caramelised in a shallow pan then mixed with the top layer that has been boiled. Finally it is placed in a clay pot to ferment for several days until ready to drink.

Historians must speculate about early brewing procedures. They theorise that bread cakes formed from germinated grains were soaked in hot water warmed by submerged heated stones. Flavour and sugar leached into the water. Yeasts fermented the sugar and a few days later it became a lowish-alcohol beer with a texture similar to soupy porridge, which needed to be filtered. Even after filtering, the cloudy brew still had solids floating around in it, so something else was required for a pleasurable drinking experience. Enter, the straw. Hollow reeds were the perfect tool for sipping the delectable potation and there are numerous contemporaneous images depicting small groups supping beer through straws poking out of large earthenware jars. These include Neolithic rock paintings found in a cave in the Algerian mountains of the Sahara, dating back to 3000 BCE or earlier, and images on Mesopotamian clay seals (*circa* 3850 BCE). They imply that imbibing beer has always been a pleasurable, convivial activity. High-status citizens like Queen Pu-abi of the city-state Ur had their own decorative straws. Pu-abi died around 2450 BCE and archaeologists unearthed from her tomb a 1-metre-long gold foil and lapis lazuli straw protruding from a large silver beer pot placed

THE ORIGIN OF THE TERM 'BARMY'

'**D**aft as a barm cake' is a phrase spoken in the north of England, especially Lancashire. It originated from the word 'barmy', to describe someone who is excitable or foolish. Barm is also another term for the yeast froth on fermented drinks and, as ale yeast is the same strain as most bakers' yeasts, it is used for baking bread, including rolls known as barm cakes.

there for her refreshment in the spirit realm. This ornate artefact can be viewed at Philadelphia's Penn Museum.

Clues to the understanding of ancient brewing are scarce due to a dearth of archaeological remains, but once again thanks to the Sumerians we have pointers in the guise of a praise poem called *A Hymn to Ninkasi* written sometime around 1800 BCE. It is composed with repeated lines, suggesting it was meant to be sung, possibly as a call and response. Not only is it a detailed description of how they brewed, but it is also the oldest existing recipe anywhere in the world, and explains how bread was baked with sweet aromatics and soaked with warm water. Sweet aromatics might refer to fruit or spices added for flavour and/or an additional supply of fermentable sugar. When Ninkasi pours the filtered beer it is described as the onrush of the Tigris and Euphrates rivers. At the time hops were not used in brewing; however, it was commonplace for Egyptians to chew bitter plants when they drank beer, and as they had taken inspiration from Sumer culture, the chances are Sumerians did the same to balance the sweetness of the malt.

Latter-day brewers have tried to replicate archaic brews, most notably San Francisco's Anchor Brewing Company, when in 1989 they followed the instructions outlined in *A Hymn To Ninkasi*, making conjectures about ingredients where the translation was inconclusive. Two versions were created and the one that most resembled beer as we know it now was around 4 per cent alcohol, brown and cloudy, with a toasty, caramel base, sherryish notes and flavours of honey and dates.

In modern craft brewing hops are the sexy beasts, with brewers naming beers after individual varieties; for example, Citra and Mosaic. The irony is that hops are not essential and brewers managed for millennia without them. Malt rarely gets a look-in even though it is the reason beer is beer. To date, the earliest written proof of a connection

between hops and brewing is from 822 CE at a Benedictine monastery in France. Several centuries later Abbess Hildegard von Bingen wrote in her natural history book *Physica Sacra*, published *circa* 1150, about the hop: '... as a result of its own bitterness it keeps some putrefactions from drinks, to which it may be added so that they may last so much longer.'

What did brewers use before hops were discovered to be so useful? Herbs, spices, fruit and honey were added for flavouring, and selected plants are bitter and have anti-bacterial properties, but even so, with limited preservative options, early brewers needed to brew regularly. In medieval Europe the botanical flavouring mixture was known as 'gruit' (alternatively gruut, gruyt, grut) and usually contained yarrow, sweet gale, rosemary and heather, and sometimes caraway, cinnamon and ginger. Gruit ale was highly intoxicating due to the narcotic and psychotropic effects of specific herbs and spices rendered even more

JURASSIC YEAST

Can there be any doubt about the awesome power of yeast? In 1995, Cuban-American microbiologist Dr Raul Cano extracted the digestive-tract contents of a bee encased in fossilised tree sap. He soaked the material in a nutritious solution and, within a week, invisible yeasts became active. Despite having been trapped in amber and lying dormant for up to forty million years, the yeast (similar to the strain commonly used to make ale) now works in a craft brewery called Fossil Fuel Brewing Co., diligently fermenting malt sugars and converting them to alcohol.

potent when fermented. Hopped beer on the other hand had the effect of sedating drinkers. In southern Germany, hops were already familiar in brewing by 1516 when Wilhelm IV, Duke of Bavaria, issued a decree that declared beer could only be made from water, barley and hops, amended decades later to include yeast when its crucial role was understood. Up until then the Catholic Church had

had a lucrative monopoly on the provision of gruit. Hops were a threat to Church revenues but, as one of the most powerful entities, it acted to influence governing authorities in its bailiwick, issuing edicts against hops and threatening to penalise brewers who used them. It was a losing battle, however, and following the Protestant Reformation, the Church's power faded and the popularity of hopped beer spread across the continent.

And what of yeast, the microscopic fungi underpinning the global drinks industry? Yeasts are extraordinary organisms dispersed in the wild by travelling on the wind as they search for food (sugar). They are found almost everywhere on Earth, even in the intestines of warm-blooded creatures. Humans have had a relationship with yeast since *Homo sapiens* evolved, but despite thousands of years of purposely crafting intoxicating drinks it was only in 1857 when scientist Louis Pasteur knew enough to explain its role in alcohol. Before then, fermentation was believed to be a gift from the gods: known in early English as 'Godisgood', the pale frothy matter which appeared after brewing was seemingly a supernatural transformation that materialised from nowhere. Over time, brewers unwittingly domesticated yeast by saving some of the foamy substance and pitching it into successive brews.

Even though no one understood the science behind fermentation, they suspected the bubbling suds were the catalyst for alcohol. Brewers used other tricks to facilitate

NEAR BEER

No- and low-alcohol beers used to be a joke because so many of them had the taste and texture of cardboard ('near beer' was a pejorative term to describe them). But that is no longer the case, and the sector is growing rapidly because there are now so many delicious options. There is no globally accepted definition of no-/low-alcohol beer, but to achieve such classification in Britain it must contain no more than 0.5 per cent alcohol. To put it into context, four ripe bananas contain a similar amount, whereas dental mouthwash can be up to 20 per cent.

There are several methods of removing alcohol, and the most successful at maintaining beeriness are filtration and vacuum distillation. Some brewers do not remove the alcohol afterwards; instead they produce wort low on fermentable sugars and employ a lazy yeast so potential alcohol strength is never going to be high.

With the canny addition of aromatic and flavoursome hops or dark malts, and oats or lactose sugars to bulk up the body, it is sometimes hard to tell the difference between beers with alcohol and those without. The disappointing days of 'near beer' are over.

fermentation; for example, creating crevices on the inside of clay pots for yeast cells to hibernate in from one brew to another. Others would stir the brew with a stick used previously so the wood became impregnated with millions of yeast cells that started fermenting when next in contact with sugary wort. This technique is still utilised in regions where beer is not produced in industrial breweries, and intricately carved wooden totems, home to their own yeast colonies, are treasured relics passed down the generations the way bakers nurture a sourdough starter and keep it in the clan for centuries.

BOCK BEER

PERSONALITY TRAITS

Picture a Venn diagram. Each of the three interlocking circles contains one of the following terms: Ale, Lager, Wild Fermentation. These are branches of the family tree of beer. Where the circles overlap, the headline is BEER. Each branch then contains sub-branches, which are the various beer styles. Ale includes Porter, Saison, Barley Wine and dozens in addition. Lager incorporates Pilsner, Schwartzbier, Bock and several more. Wild fermentation comprises Lambic, Gueuze, Faro and others, all acidic and sour and often mistaken in blind tasting for cider or wine – very useful for converting a person who claims not to enjoy beer!

The brewing process is similar for all beers, but the reason they belong to a specific branch is the strain of yeast employed during fermentation. Ale brewers commonly use a cultured strain from the *Saccharomyces cerevisiae* species. As it ferments it imparts fruity or spicy compounds called esters. Up to 50 per cent of the flavour of ale comes from the yeast, so for brewers with their own house yeast, it is the

BEER GAZETTEER

Dividing beers into styles is a sensible method of cataloguing and understanding them. Beer styles are so entrenched in the language of brewing and marketing that it may be a surprise to know the word 'style' was only used to describe beer in the late 1970s, when the seminal book *The World Guide to Beer* by beer aficionado Michael Jackson was published. Before then beers were referred to as types, species, kinds and varieties. He classified existing beers and gave labels to uncategorised Belgian ales. Thanks to Michael Jackson, consumers now understand what to expect from a beer style and are able to make educated buying choices.

equivalent of a unique flavour fingerprint. Lager brewers use *Saccharomyces pastorianus* (named in honour of Louis Pasteur), a strain that ferments slowly at a cool temperature so the esters typical of ale are not usually apparent. It also consumes one of the sugars ignored by ale yeast, resulting in beer with a crisp and light body.

Brewers who choose to ferment the traditional way, inviting spontaneous fermentation by anonymous yeast spores, would make brewers using cultured yeast tremble at the thought of feral microflora inveigling its way into the brew and bequeathing unpredictable aromas and flavours. For wild fermentation brewers this is part of the excitement and a reminder that untamed yeast is non-conformist.

Beer styles are determined by the type and balance of ingredients, colour, age and the amount of alcohol. A number of beer styles are so similar it can be difficult to tell them apart. For instance, Brown Ale and Munich Dunkel are both gently bitter and dominated by caramel and nuttiness, but Dunkel is a lager. Without sampling them together and being able to compare the body (lagers are lighter than ales) it is tricky to tell the difference. A German wheat beer may have comparable yeast-derived aromatics to its Belgian counterpart, but the latter also contains orange peel and coriander seeds, so it is a style in its own right. Sour beers can be even more confusing because not all sours stem from wild fermentation. Take Berliner Weisse, for instance. Its tang derives from the addition of *Lactobacillus* bacteria during brewing, but primary fermentation is with cultured ale yeast. Such beers are known as mixed fermentation but classed as ales. Belgian Abbey beers are categorised as 'dubbel' and 'tripel' due to their alcohol level, and this terminology has been adopted by craft brewers overseas, who use the terms double, triple and even quadruple to describe beer strength. 'Imperial' is another expression for describing alcohol and is especially used with Porter, Stout and India Pale Ale (IPA).

Why are beer styles important? Because they are a guide when deciding what to buy, in the same way that knowledge of grape varieties helps a person to choose their preferred wine. Additionally, they are required as parameters for judges to follow in beer competitions. There are currently more than 100 beer styles, and the list will grow as craft brewers develop hybrids or iterations of existing beers, which then become fashionable and widely copied.

A major influence on beer styles was an innovation in malting procedure in seventeenth-century England when a new fuel was developed. Coke (derived from coal) burns without emitting noxious fumes and was used as indirect heat for malting, replacing charcoal or wood, which imparted smokiness into the grain and often inadvertently roasted it so only dark-coloured beers were possible. The introduction of coke meant that pale malts tasting purely of cereal were possible, and this prompted the emergence of new beers.

Some styles have centuries-long staying power. A good example is India Pale Ale; it originated in the eighteenth century and has evolved over the years. Others were not so resilient and can only be found in history books; for

WALTHAM BRO'S Brewers

STOCKWELL, LONDON S.W.

PURE ENGLISH BEERS

The "HALF-GUINEA" ALE 2/6 per Doz.
"S.N." Stout 3/3 per Doz.
"Two-and Six" Stout 2/6 per Doz.

In Corked & Screw-Stoppered Bottles.

LA FORCE

LIST OF PRICES

IN CASKS

INDIA PALE ALE	54/-	27/-	10/6	5/3
THE "HALF-GUINEA" ALE	42/-	21/-	10/6	4/3
AK LIGHT BITTER ALE				
XXXX STRONG ALE (OLD OR MILD)	36/-	18/-	9/-	4/6
XXX MILD ALE	56/-	33/-	15/3	8/6
XX MILD ALE	46/-	23/-	11/3	5/9
X MILD ALE	38/-	19/-	9/-	4/6
DOUBLE STOUT	33/-	18/-	8/-	4/6
S. N. STOUT	62/-	31/-	15/6	7/6
PORTER	50/-	25/-	10/6	6/3
	38/-	18/-	9/6	4/6

TERMS.— Cash with Order, or on Delivery, subject to a DISCOUNT off all Beers, except the "Half-Guinea" Ale, of 2s. per Barrel, 1s. per Kil. 6d. per Firkin, 3d. per Pin.

BRANCHES:
Brighton, 144 Western Rd.
Croydon, 107 Parsons' Mead.
Richmond, Grosvenor Buildings.

"No Beer beats Waltham's; the 'Half-Guinea Ale' is by far the best 2/6 Beer on the market." This is everybody's verdict. All Wine Merchants and Licensed Grocers sell Waltham's Bottled Beers. The Beers are bottled at the Brewery. For Cask Beer send direct to the Brewery, or to the nearest Branch as above. Be careful not to address orders to the wrong Brewery; nor allow yourself to be wheedled into buying any other Beer.

Brewery address above — copy this.

instance, the English medieval unhopped Devonshire White Ale, a thick-textured potion that contained egg whites, had ceased to be produced by the late nineteenth century. There are still styles brewed today named after cities, towns, or their purpose: Vienna and Dortmunder lagers celebrate the places of their birth; Gose, a sour-salty wheat beer originated in the German town of Goslar; Saison, meaning 'season' in French, was originally a farm-house ale to refresh agricultural workers in Belgium's Wallonia region. Other beers are made for particular times of the year, with Winter Ales appearing in cooler months. Compared to the nomenclature of beers from great brewing civilisations of history, those monikers are prosaic. Sumerians brewed 'Beer from the World Below', 'Horned Beer' and 'Beer of Sacrifice' for ceremonial occasions. Egyptians imbibed the 'Beautiful and Heavenly', 'Friends' Beer' and 'Beer of the Protector'. Guardians of the shrine of Osiris drank 'Beer of Truth'. Special beers called 'Beer of Eternity' and 'Beer That Does Not Sour' were placed in tombs for the enjoyment of the deceased. No one knows how they tasted, but if they were as wondrous as their titles suggest then they were liquid poetry.

People who think that unless beer is composed solely of water, malt, hops and yeast then it is not really beer – or that adding tonka beans and vanilla pods is a new-fangled gim-mick – may be unaware that adding spices, fruit and other plant materials to beer is nothing new. Among the oldest

WHAT IS CRAFT BEER?

God Bless America, for without her the modern beer sector would not be so exciting. The Craft Beer Revolution happened initially in the USA when, after home-brewing was legalised in 1979, a group of beer lovers eschewed the bland pale lagers that had dominated the domestic market since Prohibition ended in 1933 and instead started to brew full-flavoured beers inspired by European styles. Ever since, craft brewers have been driven by innovation and they create thrillingly imaginative brews with dazzling aromas and flavours.

Craft beer is not a style; the description refers more to an attitude where beer is a precious drink to savour, not an industrial commodity churned out in huge volume to augment a corporation's bottom line. There is no legal definition of the phrase, and in the early days it meant microbreweries and their types of beer – usually highly hopped and/or with extra ingredients, such as coffee and black pepper – and the intention of the brewers to create the best beer possible without sacrificing flavour for the sake of production costs. Craft brewers are responsible for reviving moribund styles; for example, Grodziskie (aka Grätzer), an historic smoked wheat beer from the Polish town of Grodzisk Wielkopolski. It almost became extinct during the years of Communism but is now made by a handful of brewers in Poland and the USA.

Independent brewers globally have been inspired by the no-rules approach of American craft brewers, and drinkers are the beneficiaries, with access to a range and variety of beers like never before. Unfortunately, the phrase 'craft beer' is becoming meaningless now it has been purloined by large corporations as a marketing term, often to sell the types of ordinary beer responsible for motivating the original craft beer revolution.

evidence of a fermented cereal drink is the 9,000-year-old residue on clay pots discovered in a Neolithic village in China. It contained rice, honey, grapes and possibly hawthorn. Modern-day craft brewers producing 'blueberry maple syrup pancake lassi Mild' have as much right to call it beer as the brewer of a pint of traditional Bitter does. As long as the majority of fermentable sugars derive from cereal and the brew has not been distilled, then it is beer.

TASTING BEER LIKE A BOSS

Describing a beer as having 'coffee, treacle and liquorice flavours' or 'a crisp and light body with subtle herbal aroma and soft biscuit malt character' is not unusual now, but before the mid-1980s there was no tasting vocabulary for beer. Wine had a rudimentary lexicon from at least the first century CE when Pliny the Elder wrote of wines tasting luscious, or harsh, unripe, sharp and rough.

A brewing flavour wheel was developed in the 1970s by American chemist Dr Morten Meilgaard and his colleagues, with brief terms to describe the range of aromas and flavours in beer. This was accessible for brewers but was not widely available to consumers. It was only when esteemed British beer writers Roger Protz and the late Michael Jackson, sitting in a London pub one night, described their pint of Everard's Tiger Bitter as being 'nutty' that they were inspired to collate descriptive notes of the beers they wrote about. Initially, many did not understand the concept and thought it was a joke to say a beer had chocolate flavours, especially when at the time descriptions no more

THE INFLUENCE OF GLASSWARE

Before glassware became affordable in Britain through mass-production methods and a tax reduction on glass in the nineteenth century, beer was consumed from a variety of vessels. Through the centuries they included mugs fashioned from wood, clay, pewter or leather; shallow wooden bowls called mazars usually attached to a broad flat pedestal; and hollow animal horns with a pointed end. In some rural parts of Africa, communal beer drinking through straws from capacious earthenware jars is still the way to imbibe, but try swirling one of them to release the aromas! Modern glass shapes influence the drinking experience in the following ways:

☞ A conical chimney leading from the bowl concentrates aroma and directs it to the nose.

- ☞ A narrow neck circumference means beer is sipped, thereby influencing the flow of liquid over the tongue and enhancing flavour.
- ☞ Bowl surface area impacts the degree of exposure to air. This allows the beer to breathe and is important for big aromatics.
- ☞ Wheat beer foam heads are accentuated by a tall, slender glass flared at the top.
- ☞ Wide-mouthed glasses encourage glugging, which means the beer hits the back of the tongue and is swallowed before the aromas and flavours register properly.

enlightening than 'beery' were routine. Eventually people saw the value of knowing beforehand how a beer would taste so they could decide whether or not to buy. Roger Protz and Michael Jackson have elevated the reputation of beer in myriad ways, and their decision to use wine phraseology has been adopted worldwide. It is rare now to find a beer that does not have even the most basic flavour descriptions.

Sensory experts have identified thousands of aroma and flavour compounds because of the diversity of water, malt, hops, yeast, and adjuncts including fruit and spices. How about this for a mouth-watering melange? From malt: biscuits, brown bread, caramel, cereal, chocolate, coffee, honey, nuts, smokiness, bacon, toast, tobacco, toffee. From hops: citrus, herbal, grassy, peach, pineapple, lychee, passion fruit, floral, pine, woody, peppery, spicy. From yeast and other microflora: bubblegum, banana, raisins, berry and stone fruit, citrus, spice, balsamic vinegar.

Beer can offer some of the most complex drinking experiences. Those who are happy chugging without giving much thought will still enjoy it, but individuals who want to think while they drink should prepare to be surprised. To get the most out of beer entails mindfulness, at least for the opening few sips, as all the senses are engaged. A beer gulped and swallowed quickly has no time to disclose itself fully and the drinker will just have a basic overview comprised mostly of texture and bitterness, missing out on the panoply of other characteristics.

Appearance, the sound as it is poured, how it tastes, and sensations in the mouth all add to the pleasure. Foam is important because it enhances visual impact. It is unique to beer and is caused by an interaction between malt proteins, a compound in hops, and air bubbles. Wheat beer foam

BLIND TASTING ALTERS PERCEPTION

Humans make value judgements within seconds, especially visual ones. Some people claim not to enjoy dark beers, but in a scientific research project where the colour was obscured, the volunteer guinea pigs could not discern any difference between the pale and the dark beers, even though beforehand, when they had tasted the same beers and could see the colour, they noted different flavours. Proof that ocular clues influence a person's expectations.

is more voluptuous than that on beer made from 100 per cent barley because of the extra protein in wheat. Draught Guinness usually has a solid head because of the high percentage of nitrogen gas injected as it is served. How tight or loose the head is will affect the aromas emanating from the beer. If it is loose then they can escape, whereas if it is tight they gather under the head.

An ideal-shaped vessel is a snifter (also known as a balloon) made from thin glass so the beer is in intimate contact with the mouth. It has a bulbous bowl, giving a large surface area for aromas to develop, and it narrows towards the rim where the aromas congregate and are funnelled to the nose. Smell is the most important factor in beer tasting because the brain registers 80 per cent of flavours through millions of olfactory cells. Sense of smell is powerful when it comes to recollection. Years after the fact it has the power to transport a person's imagination back to a terrible hangover. Aroma can prompt positive or negative responses because the olfactory system is part of the limbic network;

it connects to the amygdala, the area of the brain where emotion is processed, and to the hippocampus, which is concerned with experiences and learning through association. No other sense has that intimate connection with memory. Let's hear it for the nose!

So how do you taste your beer like a pro? Fill the glass about one-third full and then swirl it to release the aromas. Sniff a couple of times and try and describe the smell. Take a sip, and as it travels over the tongue, it warms, and aromatic vapours infuse into the nasal cavity where cells communicate flavour components to the brain. Receptors in several thousand taste buds gather molecules and send messages to the brain about levels of sour, sweet, salt, bitter and umami (savoury) tastes. After swallowing, immediately breathe out through the nose and even more flavours will be revealed. This is called retro-nasal olfaction.

Think about the body of the beer: is it light, medium or full? Is the alcohol apparent? Alcohol has a warming effect and the higher it is, the sweeter and smoother the beer will be because alcohol balances astringency. What is the texture – drying, tannic, smooth, prickly with carbonation? Carbonation increases acidity and concentrates bitterness, so the bigger the carbonation, the drier and more bitter the beer will be. Consider the balance – is it harmonious, or is one factor (or more) standing out to the detriment of enjoyment? There is a lot to analyse when professionally tasting beer, so don't do it in one mouthful; repeat the exercise several times.

PERFECT PARTNERS

'BEER ON the dining table? How *declassé*. The correct way is to dine with wine.' Anyone who holds that opinion is one or more of the following: a public relations director for the wine industry; a person who does not realise beer can be served in elegant glassware, not just pint glasses; or someone who is unaware that beer is the most diverse of all alcoholic drinks and has ample potential for matching with food.

Beer has a plethora of flavours, tastes and textures. It goes with all cuisines, and all items on the menu whether vegan, vegetarian, fish or meat, from breakfast to post-dinner dessert. Because of beer's reputation as the beverage for everyone, and the heritage of wine as a status drink, many believe the latter to be the 'proper' choice when dining. In Anglophone countries where beer is usually served in unattractive pint glasses with crisps as the accompaniment, the majority opinion is that beer suits casual meals but is inappropriate for fine dining. Travel to Belgium, however, and it is unthinkable that beer would not be judged worthy of serving in chalices with haute cuisine.

When choosing what to pair with wine, it is not necessary to think of what goes with grapes, and with beer there is no need to find a match for barley. When considering a successful pairing for wine, acidity, tannins, sweetness and body are the devices. Beer has all those too, plus bitterness, umami and even salt. It is mostly composed of water (refreshing) and contains carbonation in varying degrees from gentle through to moussey, effervescent and prickly. Combined, all these properties give beer an advantage over other beverages when dining. Why?

Carbon dioxide A by-product of fermentation dissolved in the beer. Often beer is also additionally carbonated. CO_2 cuts through texture and scrubs the palate.

Acidity Refreshing and balances rich flavours. It is also a palate cleanser. Hops contain acids; sour beers contain acidic-tasting microflora. Carbon dioxide creates acidity through carbonic acid, giving beer a refreshing 'bite'.

Tannins Compounds derived from plant material. With beer they come from cereals and hops. Tannins add texture and structure to beer. Their ability to attract fats and proteins and separate them means they cut through the texture of dense or fatty food and refresh the mouth.

Hops Contain acids, tannins, aroma and flavour. They are also bitter, which is refreshing and provides a contrast to other tastes in the meal, thereby creating a balance of flavours.

Malt Contains tannins, acidity, sweetness and a range of flavours to complement the food.

Before we start, we need a bitter aperitif. A gin and tonic would be good but, as this is a book about beer, choose Pale Ale instead. There is a practical reason: when the tongue senses bitterness the hormone gastrin is released and starts digestive operations. Enzymes in saliva convert starches into easily digestible carbohydrates. A message is then sent to the stomach, where hydrochloric acid is secreted in order to break down the soon-to-arrive comestibles. The small intestine now prompts the liver to produce bile and the gall bladder to manage bile excretion – bile assists the liver in breaking down fats and ridding the body of waste products. Finally, inside the pancreas insulin is produced to regulate blood sugar. Bitter ale prompted this cascade of digestive processes. A plateful of rocket would have the same effect, but beer is more fun!

If only Queen Elizabeth II served beer at official events, then the notion of wine being the only appropriate drink for dining would immediately change. Imagine eating this feast from a real state banquet hosted by the Queen for the

French president. She served wine, but in our imaginary collation we have exquisite beers instead.

- ☞ Paupiette de Sole et Gresson, sauce Nantua (sole with crayfish sauce) with Belgian Witbier. The beer has a creamy texture and a subtle citrus note that complements the delicate texture and flavour of the fish.
- ☞ Agneau de la Nouvelle Saison de Windsor au Basilic (new Windsor lamb) with oak-aged Barley Wine. The caramel flavour in the beer harmonises with the sweetness educed by roasting the meat, and the tannins and carbonation cut through the texture.
- ☞ Charlotte à la Vanille et Cerises Griottes (creamy cherry dessert) with Kriek. The beer contains sour cherries to complement the dessert, and its refreshing acidity cuts through the creamy texture.

England's sixteenth-century queen, Elizabeth I, was a keen ale drinker, even for breakfast when she was reputed to consume a quart (approximately 2 pints) with mutton or beef stew and manchet, the finest wheaten bread. If that sounds like party time at the palace, it wasn't. Ale and bread for breakfast were commonplace in the medieval era. English ale of the period was often brown and malty with a smoky flavour and a thick texture, a perfect match for the pottage.

GUIDELINES FOR BEER AND FOOD MATCHING

While there are no strict rules with pairing, there are some useful guidelines and tips you can follow.

Texture Think about the texture of the food when choosing the beer; for instance, with salad or sushi, a Helles lager rather than a hefty tripel Abbey beer would be a better match.

Flavour intensity Pair the beer with the flavour intensity of the food. Game is highly flavoured and needs a big beast like Dopplebock to match, whereas that same beer would overwhelm poached cod.

Main part of the dish Partner the beer with the main part of the dish rather than the accompaniments, unless it is a curry, in which case think about the piquancy of the sauce. Sunday roast has many elements, so ignore the peas when choosing the beer; pair instead with the meat/nut loaf. A malty Scotch Ale would be complementary.

Colour If in doubt, match the colour of the beer to the food; for example, grilled chicken with Golden Ale. Using colour as a guide works with wine, and the same goes for beer.

Cooking method Whether food is steamed, fried, grilled or roasted affects flavour and texture. A marvellous complementary match would be smoked beer with smoked fish, for example.

Alcohol as a flavour enhancer Higher-alcohol beers will intensify flavours in the food and can unbalance it. Spicy dishes are spicier with high alcohol.

Saltiness This increases bitterness in beer. Sweeter beers are better with salty foods because they contrast.

Bitter foods These taste more intense with bitter beers. Choose a beer sweeter than the food.

Spicy foods Avoid bitter-flavoured beers if you don't want to increase the intensity of the spices and overpower the dish.

Sweet foods These work best with bitter and/or roasted flavours in beer as a contrast.

A USEFUL MANTRA

Co-ordinate Choose a beer to match the texture and density of the food.

Cut Choose a beer to cut through texture and richness and reveal the flavours.

Complement Choose a beer to complement the food flavours.

Contrast Choose a beer to contrast with the food; for instance a sweet beer with salty food.

Elizabeth employed both beer and ale brewers when there was still a distinction between the two beverages, with beer being bitter and hopped, and ale being neither. The diet of affluent Tudors was meat-focused, so tannins in the beer would have had a better chance than ale of cutting through the texture of the game, goose, swan, peacock, beef, lamb, mutton, pork and other provisions that adorned the dining tables of the wealthy. When Gloriana went on royal progresses around her realm, if the host's ale and beer were not up to scratch, then the Queen's brewers were despatched to supply the household for the duration of her stay.

Historically ale and, later, beer were staples consumed with every meal, and in between too, although there was no concept of pairing with specific dishes. Water was not trusted and until the prices of imported tea and coffee were reduced in Britain in the nineteenth century, making it affordable to people on low incomes, there were few alternatives for liquid refreshment. In the Victorian era most English restaurants stocked beer, and it was customary for diners to order a glass with their meal. Even into the early twentieth century it was so common to have beer with a repast that breweries delivered small casks of lowish-alcohol Dinner Ale to private homes for the family to drink at mealtimes. When the reusable screw-cap bottle was invented in 1879, this packaging format was even more convenient for the table.

Arguably the best-known beer pairing is oysters with Porter or Stout. It's hard to believe, now they are a status dish, that until the end of the nineteenth century, oysters were inexpensive street food. As a character commented in Charles Dickens' novel *The Pickwick Papers*, 'poverty and oysters always seem to go together'. So did Porter, the low-cost option for beer. If the Victorians had chosen beers to go with their meal they could have looked forward to a bill of fare like this: London Particular (pea soup) served with light Mild – the beer has low bitterness and a malty base enhanced by the ham hock in the soup; Steak and Kidney Pudding with Bitter – the beer is well hopped to cut through the texture but has a sweet, malty base that contrasts with the savoury meat; Spotted Dick with Old Ale – the dried fruit flavours of both pudding and beer are complementary.

CAKES AND ALE

Cakes do indeed go fabulously well with ale. The phrase will be familiar to scholars of William Shakespeare's *Twelfth Night* when Sir Toby Belch says to Malvolio, 'Dost thou think, because thou art virtuous, there shall be no more cakes and ale?', referring, in this context, to pleasure and the good things in life.

Proof of the pudding is in the eating and drinking, so if you do not believe that cake with beer is one of nature's greatest rewards, then try these combinations:

☞ Eton mess with Frambozen, the sour Belgian fruit beer. The acidity of the beer balances the richness of the meringue and cream, and the raspberry in the beer complements the fruit in the pudding.

☞ Lemon drizzle cake with Lime Berliner Weissbier. A luscious sweet and sour contrast.

☞ Tiramisu with Double Chocolate Stout. The beer has bitterness to contrast with the sweetness, and chocolate as a complement.

☞ Sticky toffee pudding with Red Ale. Both beer and dessert are dominated by caramel, so they complement each other, and the bitterness of the ale is a contrast to the sweetness of the dessert.

And then there's the cheese. Ooh la la! If ever a libation and foodstuff were destined to be together they are beer and cheese. Some beer and cheese matches are transformative: try a funky and salty blue Stilton with Imperial Russian Stout and its massive treacle, coffee and liquorice flavours; soft earthy Brie with a bone-dry Saison, its acidity cutting through the unctuous texture; tangy goat's cheese with a creamy Weizen; or the mouth-watering umami taste of Lincolnshire Poacher with the Dundee-fruit-cake character of an aged Barley Wine.

It is serendipity, because not only did the first written account of beer originate in Sumer, so did the earliest known mention of cheese, recorded on clay tablets and dating to between 2094 and 2047 BCE (the Third Dynasty of Ur). Sumerians made around twenty types of cheese from cow's, ewe's and goat's milk. Imagining them making a decision about what cheese they were in the mood for with one of their special-occasion brews such 'Beer from the World Below' is a delicious thought.

TO YOUR GOOD HEALTH

Santé, *gesondheid* and *sláinte* are all words that translate roughly as 'health' and are used when toasting and saying 'cheers'. The association with health and alcohol is deep-rooted because humans have used it for aeons as a delivery method for medicinal botanicals, as a painkiller and sterilant, and for the advantages ethanol itself offers, most notably in reducing the risk of heart disease and stroke. There are some genuine health benefits to alcoholic drinks (in moderation and with caveats) – just what the doctor ordered.

Contemporary medical advice on alcohol varies from country to country, but the received wisdom is that over-consumption can have adverse effects on health. Which is why the long-running but now mothballed marketing strapline for Mackeson Milk Stout – 'Looks good, tastes good and by golly it does you good' – would never be permitted by the Advertising Standards Authority today. Yet beer is arguably more benign than other alcoholic beverages because of its combination of ingredients, each beneficial to health.

MACKESON'S milk STOUT
DOES YOU <u>DOUBLE</u> GOOD

NOW, more than ever before, you need the *double goodness* of Mackeson's Milk Stout. A Mackeson's puts new heart, new energy into you. Each bottle contains the energising carbohydrates of pure dairy milk as well as malt, hops and yeast. You get the energy of stout *plus* the energy of milk. That's why doctors say Mackeson's does you *double good*. Have a Mackeson's today and keep those wartime troubles at arm's length!

At all Whitbread 'houses' and off-licences and at leading retailers everywhere.

Malted cereal contains proteins, carbohydrates, minerals, vitamins, amino acids and soluble fibre. It is especially rich in the B-complex vitamins (so is brewers' yeast) essential in almost every process in the body, including energy production, digestion, the central nervous system, and for healthy hair, skin and nails. One of the essential minerals supplied by beer is silicon, which derives from the husk of the cereal and helps maintain healthy joints and bone density. Medical studies concluded that beer drinkers were less likely to suffer from osteoporosis than non-drinkers, and the presence of silicon was one reason. Silicon is vital for the formation of collagen, the protein found in blood vessel walls, tendons and skin. Beer is the biggest dietary source of the mineral, and one pint contains over half the recommended daily intake. When food and drink is fermented, its nutritional value increases in a transformation known as biological ennoblement, so the malt in beer is much more nutritious than it would be as breakfast cereal.

Most sugars from malt are fermented out as they convert to alcohol. In small quantities, alcohol can reduce the threat of coronary heart disease by raising the amount of 'good' cholesterol (high-density lipoprotein), and lowering the risk of arteriosclerosis (hardening of the arteries). Alcohol is a vasodilator, meaning it dilates blood vessels, leading to unimpeded flow and ideal pressure.

Yeast provides a plethora of health benefits too – just ensure the beer is unfiltered and unpasteurised so the yeast is still present as it is with real ale and bottle-conditioned beer. In addition to being nutritionally dense – containing protein, chromium, potassium, copper, selenium, iron, zinc and B-complex vitamins – yeast strengthens the immune system and is probiotic, making it useful for treating digestive-tract disorders like irritable bowel syndrome. Brewers' yeast has been used for decades in herbal medicine for its tonic, antiseptic and stimulant properties, and to treat respiratory problems, seasonal allergies and type 2 diabetes. It has a positive effect on diabetes because it contains the highest glucose tolerance factor (GTF) of any food. GTF is a dietary essential as it enhances the effect of insulin in utilising glucose efficiently to maintain optimum blood sugar levels.

IS STOUT ANY HEALTHIER THAN OTHER BEER STYLES?

Stout has a reputation for being wholesome and restorative, yet it contains no more goodness than any other beer. The connection between good health and Stout was firmly established in the public's mind by the end of the nineteenth century when doctors prescribed it as a pick-me-up tonic, for nursing mothers, and as easy-to-obtain nourishment for patients with no appetite or suffering from wasting disease. Brewers capitalised on this repute. 'Guinness is Good For You' was a familiar slogan in the early to mid-twentieth century, and because of that simple and memorable message, Stout is still considered to be particularly healthful.

Hops, or 'little wolf', as a rough translation of their Latin species name *Humulus lupulus* suggests, are anything but wolf-like. 'Pharmacy of the fields' would be more accurate because they can be used to treat a variety of complaints; for example, insomnia, tension, migraine and indigestion. They help to prevent calcium leaching from the bones which, unchecked, is a cause of kidney stones and osteoporosis. Hops have a sedative effect and are used in herbal sleeping tablets. A beneficial substance in hops is a flavonoid called xanthohumol. It has anti-inflammatory, antioxidant and anticancer effects and may combat the progression of chronic liver disease. Hops can inhibit the growth of *Helicobacter pylori* bacteria, the cause of infection connected with stomach cancer and gastric and duodenal ulcers. Hops contain the second-highest amount (after soya) of the micronutrient phyto-oestrogen, and consequently natural hormone replacement therapy supplements contain hop extracts. Consumption of phyto-oestrogen is also connected with a decreased incidence of breast cancer in humans.

Before hops were used in brewing, there were other anti-bacterial compounds connected with beer. Anthropologist George Armelagos and chemist Mark Nelson analysed the bones of residents of Nubia (Sudan) who had lived between 350 and 550 CE, and discovered they contained concentrated amounts of tetracycline, an antibiotic generated by *Streptomyces* bacteria during fermentation. The scientists concluded the source of the *Streptomyces* was the soil in which Nubians grew the cereal to make their beer.

Now that modern medicine claims to know most of the answers, the wisdom of our ancestors is often dismissed. The habit of our great-grandmothers for sipping beer before breastfeeding their babies because it helped milk to flow may be scorned as an old wives' tale, but it is a cross-cultural tradition practised at least as long ago as the Sumerian era (third to fifth millennia BCE). Beer had the reputation of being a galactagogue, a foodstuff thought to accelerate lactation. Antyllus, a Greek surgeon based in Rome in the second century CE, wrote of mixing earthworms and dates into beer to encourage plentiful breast milk. Scientists know now that a polysaccharide from barley and dates stimulates the secretion of prolactin, the hormone that instructs the body to lactate. Earthworms, meanwhile, still have a number of uses in Chinese medicine; for instance, expediting childbirth and promoting lactation.

Beer has been a versatile element of the medicine cabinet for centuries. In fourth-century-CE Gaul a remedy for intestinal worms was a beer- and herb-soaked suppository. Medics in medieval Europe relied on beer to soothe numerous ailments, sometimes on its own rubbed into the scalp to get rid of lice, and other times with added botanicals to treat digestive disorders. Butterbeer was the favourite drink for J. K. Rowling's young wizards, but buttered beer was a real concoction in medieval England to treat coughs and

BREWER'S DROOP

'Brewer's droop' is slang for erectile dysfunction, but is the condition connected with beer? Hops are alleged to have anaphrodisiac (the opposite to aphrodisiac) properties, but results from medical research are inconclusive. However, there is a link between alcohol abuse and the sex hormones that control the ability of a man to maintain an erection. To be fair, and not to just put the blame on beer, it should be boozer's droop!

shortness of breath. It consisted of a mixture of beer, butter, egg yolk, grated ginger and sugar.

In Scandinavian countries a traditional farmhouse beer known as Sahti includes juniper. Juniper is a coniferous tree native to the northern hemisphere and the berries, actually seed cones, are used in Sahti for flavour, and the twigs as filtering material. Juniper has legendary medicinal properties, used in folk medicine for its antibacterial, antiviral and antiseptic effects, and for treating myriad conditions including gout, arthritis, rheumatism and infections of the urinary tract and respiratory system. It also has a mystical reputation with the power to ward off bad magic and negative influences.

And what about the social benefits of beer? Communal contact is fundamental to humans, and without it a person's mental health can suffer. In 2017, research by the University of Oxford's Department of Experimental Psychology revealed that people who went to their local pub for a pint and conversation were more contented than those who did not. Drinking beer and socialising triggers endorphins that activate opiate receptors in the brain, reducing pain, boosting pleasure and resulting in a feeling of well-being.

SUPERSTAR BEERS OF THE WORLD

OF THE DOZENS of beer styles, three have had a global impact in a way none of the others have. They are Pilsner, India Pale Ale and Porter.

PILSNER

On the map of beer significance, the true epicentre is the city of Plzeň in the Czech Republic. That is the place which gave its name to the style of beer that now dominates the global brewing industry. Pilsner (sometimes spelled Pilsener) means 'from Pilsen'. At its best it is both crisp and delicate with a balance of sweet malt and grassy, floral-flavoured hops. It is the template for all industrially produced pale lagers, although most of those are poor imitations, with added enzymes to speed up production and reduce weeks-long ageing times to days. The word 'lager' comes from the German *lagern* – meaning 'store'. Brewers use the expression 'lagering' to describe the process of beer maturation.

Brown- and mahogany-coloured lagers had existed in Bavaria since the fifteenth century, when they were brewed in cool caves with a strain of yeast adapted to cold conditions. It was a hybrid of *Saccharomyces cerevisiae* and an unknown species that endowed low temperature tolerance. In 2011, scientists identified the anonymous parent when its genome matched yeast growing in a wood in Patagonia. They dubbed it *Saccharomyces eubayanus.* Where it originated is a mystery, as it has never been found in the wild in Germany. What a fortuitous marriage of strains though, because the pure cultured hybrid, now called *Saccharomyces pastorianus*, is used to ferment more than 95 per cent of the world's beers.

In 1842, Bavarian brewer Josef Groll was hired by a Plzeň-based company called Bürger Brauerei, later to be known as Pilsner Urquell (translation: 'original source of Pilsner'). He fermented a batch of beer with a sample of lager yeast from his home region. Very importantly the brewery had acquired an up-to the-minute malt kiln from England, enabling the production of pale malts, meaning golden-hued beers were possible. Such a colour for lager was unknown, so the new beer was a sensation; even more so because of its drinkability. Plzeň water was very low in mineral salts and showcased the flavours of the barley and hops grown in the surrounding countryside. The beer was matured slowly for weeks in cold subterranean cellars under the town. Unlike most beers of the time, it was clear, not hazy, and with its excellent flavour it became a hit with the local populace. Almost immediately its reputation spread and supplies were shipped by the recently built railway network to Europe's capital cities and beyond.

Refrigeration and the scientific approach taken by microbiologist Emile Hansen, who experimented at the Carlsberg brewery in Copenhagen and isolated stable strains of yeast, meant Pilsner could be produced with a consistency rare at the time. Reliability was a boon for brewers and soon the beer was made in several other European countries. Bürger Brauerei failed to trademark the term 'pilsner bier' until 1859, but by then it was too late; other breweries were using it to market their versions of the beer.

Not all countries surrendered to the nineteenth-century advance of Pilsner-style beers, however. They were

Belgium, Britain, Ireland and the region of the German Rhineland. Pale lagers were consumed in those areas but ale still reigned until the twentieth century. Both Belgium and Britain are renowned for their ale-brewing traditions and yet in both countries today pale lager easily outsells every other style. Stella Artois, one of the world's biggest-selling beers, originated in the Belgian city of Leuven.

During the nineteenth century, European brewers who emigrated to the New World were in demand to establish breweries and make the popular beers from home. Brewing companies, especially in America, started to export pale lager to Australasia, Africa and Asia, and in a canny move they usually included ice with the shipment because cold beer in hot climates is irresistible. Pilsner is the perfect unchallenging beverage – easy to drink, light, quenching, and, when carbonated, it provides super-charged spritzy refreshment. Multiple millions of pints are brewed each week to service the planet's insatiable thirst for beer.

INDIA PALE ALE

It is a fluke that the name of this beer style contains the word India, because it could have been Canada, or any number of other countries. The moniker derived from the destination of trading vessels transporting goods from Britain to the sub-continent from at least 1711. Ships carried beer as an alternative to drinking water, as nutrition for the crew, as a trading commodity, and even as ballast for empty outbound craft that would return laden with freight. There is a widely reported myth that India Pale Ale was invented specifically for the Indian market to refresh British soldiers. It is a fallacy, because the style already existed but was called October beer or October malt wine.

Not far from London's East India Dock was a brewery owned by George Hodgson. From the mid-eighteenth century he sold beer to ship captains trading with representatives of the East India Company. As well as Porter, they also bought the pale and bitter October beer. This was named after the autumnal month because until the development of central heating and refrigeration, brewers were restricted by the sensitivity of yeast to brew only in spring or autumn when the ambient temperature permitted successful fermentation. October beers were high in alcohol and intended to be aged for months, even years, in wooden barrels in order to develop complex flavours. Ageing the beer added a tart note from microflora impregnated in the wood. Hodgson's October beer was highly hopped, and hops preserve beer, so it had resilience. During the 4–6-month-long voyage the rocking action of the oceans and temperature fluctuation had the miraculous effect of speeding maturation, so on arrival in India it had the qualities of a beer aged for much longer.

Generous credit terms extended by Hodgson helped him to dominate the growing market where October beer became the premium drink of British officials. Lower-status employees and soldiers in the private armies of the East India Company continued to drink the less expensive Porter. Brewers based in the English brewing town of Burton-upon-Trent also started to make the lucrative pale beer, and by around 1829 it was being marketed as East India Pale Ale, later to be shortened to India Pale Ale. The water of the River Trent is high in calcium and magnesium sulphate and produces better Pale Ale than London's calcium carbonate-heavy water does. Trent water enhanced the properties of hops, decreased the colour from the malt, and reduced haze, producing a clear pale beer with a pronounced bitterness. Customers overseas started to notice Burton-brewed Pale Ale was superior to ales of elsewhere. The development of the railway network in 1839 connected Burton with major cities and meant beer could be transported quickly and widely. The Bass Brewery became synonymous with the town and by the late 1870s was the largest brewing company on Earth, with millions of its bottles of Pale Ale exported to Australia, New Zealand, China, USA, Chile, South Africa and over fifty other countries. It was so celebrated that Édouard Manet depicted two bottles in the bottom right and left corners of his Impressionist masterpiece *A Bar at the Folies-Bergère*. With the distinctive red triangle (the UK's trademark number 1) on the labels, they are conspicuous among the bottles of Champagne.

By the second half of the nineteenth century, Pale Ales typically had alcohol levels of around 6–7 per cent ABV, lower than October beers had been, which meant they were more quaffable so demand increased, not least in the domestic British market where the beer was nicknamed 'Bitter' to differentiate it from malty Mild and Porter. The popularity of India Pale Ale began an inexorable decline from the end of the nineteenth century, as pale lagers became the dominant style brewed worldwide. The First World War had a major impact too when the British government passed legislation to restrict the strength of beer and IPA became a whisper of its former self.

That whisper has become a roar, however, because India Pale Ale has had a remarkable renaissance. It started in 1990 when British beer lover, and later publican, Mark Dorber persuaded Roger Protz and Michael Jackson, along with brewers and hop and barley growers, to revive appreciation of the venerable beer by initiating the brewing of a 1850s Bass recipe. This was the catalyst for a small group of British and American brewers to join the renewed admiration of the style and brew their own versions of IPA. As America's Craft Beer Revolution expanded in the 1990s, IPA became the talisman of small independent brewers, who used it as a canvas for multiple layers of flavour the way Jackson Pollock applied paint. Now it is so fashionable it accounts for more than a quarter of all the beer brewed in the craft beer sector, with numerous, sometimes flamboyant, adaptations such as Tropical Fruit Milk Shake IPA that would surprise, maybe puzzle, eighteenth-century brewers of the beer. Brewers in all the countries inspired by American craft brewing pay homage to IPA, and it is now the world's most widely produced ale.

PORTER

Raise a toast to Porter, the original global beer. Porter is a savoury glassful of chocolate, coffee, nuts and molasses that began as dark and malty London Brown Ale and had a makeover to become dry, vinous and less sweet. Porter earned the soubriquet around 1721 in recognition of the street and river porters who drank gallons of it

as refreshment after days of carrying goods around or unloading freight from ships in the capital. In the eighteenth century Porter was ubiquitous. Commander James Cook's ship *Endeavour* was stocked with it during a voyage of exploration to the Pacific in 1768, and twenty years later it was the first beer in the new Australian colony. It refreshed troops in Britain's overseas territories for decades, and wherever British immigrants settled, Porter followed as a familiar taste of home. The beer turned eighteenth-century London into a brewing powerhouse. State-of the-art mechanised breweries built by Truman's, Barclay Perkins and Whitbread were awe-inspiring. Huge fortunes were accrued but large amounts of capital were required to brew it because Porter was aged for months, even years, in gigantic wooden vats and was expensive to produce. By the 1870s brewers were reluctant to spend so much money and time maturing the beer, and consequently quality and sales declined. Pale Ale was growing in reputation in Britain at the expense of Porter.

Most people have heard of Stout but not Porter, and yet without the latter, Stout as we understand it (i.e. a dark beer) would not exist. The word 'stout' was initially used around 1630 in connection with beer, when it meant 'strong'. Dr Samuel Johnson's *A Dictionary of the English Language*, published in 1755, mentioned stout as being slang for strong beer. Any high-alcohol beer, even a pale one, could be described as Stout, but as Porter dominated the market the expression came to be associated with dark beer. Stout Porter was only one iteration; others were called Common, Best, Superior and Double Porter.

When small-time Dublin brewer Arthur Guinness decided in 1799 to concentrate on brewing Porter, it was a wise move, because his eponymous company grew to become the world's best-known producer of Stout. In the

PORTER BREWER'S DRAYMEN.

Pub. by R. Ackermann, London.

nineteenth century the recipe was changed to include a high proportion of unmalted roasted barley, which gave the beer an almost black hue and a distinctive charred quality. That evolution of London Brown Ale was called Extra Stout Porter and has become a sub-style known today as Irish Dry Stout.

Porter went out of fashion in the mid-twentieth century but now has a starring role in craft brewing. The style lends itself to unions with other ingredients and flavours, with Bourbon barrel-aged, coffee and smoked being three popular iterations.

BELGIUM – A BEER LOVER'S PARADISE

OF ALL BEER-loving countries, Belgium deserves special mention. No other nation has earned the accolade of its beer culture being included on UNESCO's List of the Intangible Cultural Heritage of Humanity. What makes it worthy of this outstanding recognition? For a start Belgian beer styles are not only diverse but distinctive, from the singular palate-awakening Gueuze, so sour it should come with a warning for people expecting bitterness, and the elegant, moussey mouthfeel of Brut de Flandres, which goes through a secondary fermentation with Champagne yeast in the bottle, to the juicy cherry and raspberry tang of Kriek and Frambozen, dry-as-a-bone Saison, and the Trappist beers that are more dark and complex than any cases investigated by Hercule Poirot. Despite such diversity there is a common denominator in Belgian beers – yeast is a dominant factor in the flavour profiles. Whether it is the microflora of the Pajottenland region, home of Lambic beers, that render indescribable funkiness; Witbier yeasts with their banana- and clove-like esters; peppery Pale Ales;

or Abbey beers where the yeast ordains a potpourri of Christmas spice on the palate, they deliver an unmistakable quality to Belgian beers.

Belgium's grand cafés should be classified as one of the wonders of the world, not least for the length of their beer menus, a challenge for anyone indecisive. Delirium Café in Brussels holds the Guinness World Record for a list of just over 2,000 beers. In all Belgian cafés the beer is served in glassware designed to enhance the appearance and/or the flavour of the beer. No ugly pint glasses there! Instead, an assortment of branded chalices, tulips and snifters on stems. None can compare to the glass for Kwak beer, however. Picture an elongated Liebig condenser with an open flared neck propped up in a wooden bracket with a handle. Unsurprisingly, many overseas beer tourists covet such a unique glass as a souvenir, so one bar has implemented drastic measures. Customers must hand over a shoe when they order Kwak, and the footwear is returned when the glass is relinquished. Said bar now has a big collection of single shoes.

Arguably the type of traditional beer most associated with Belgium is that influenced by monastic brewing. Known as Abbey beers, these brews range from light to dark, dry to sweet, medium to full bodied, with alcohol up to 10 per cent, and they hark back to the time when the Catholic Church was all-powerful, with a network of monasteries. The order of Cistercian monks had a branch known as Trappists and they were particularly adept at brewing. The land now known as Belgium was in a tumultuous region where relentless war and occupation scarred society. During the French Revolution, monasteries were pillaged, bringing an end to brewing. Several decades later when Trappist monasteries were re-established, so was brewing by men of the cloth. War interrupted the making of beer in 1914 and 1940, and when it returned in the post-Second World War period some breweries with no connection to the Church started to produce beers named after saints or with images of fat, jolly monks on the label, giving the impression they were authentic Trappist Ales. To mitigate damage to their reputation, the International Trappist Association now has legal protection, so only beers brewed by or under the supervision of Trappist monks (for instance, Chimay, Westmalle and Orval) can use the term. Beers brewed in a similar style but by secular brewers are known as Abbey beers.

One style to set many a beer lover's heart fluttering is Flanders Red Ale. Tart and complex, these beers have a sherbet-mousse mouthfeel, and are laden with dried fruit, spice, orange and vinous flavours. Tannins come from ageing in foeders (huge oak barrels) for 18–24 months. They are a beer bridge for wine and cider drinkers to cross over, and when served in a blind tasting, people are usually clueless as to what drink they are sampling. Really they deserve to be a category all of their own, one titled 'Spectacular'.

It is the height of hospitality, a compliment to the good taste of guests to serve that which is acknowledged the best of its class.

Pabst
Blue Ribbon
The Beer of Quality

is the ultimate choice of all who have a keen faculty of selection.

Made and Bottled Only
by Pabst at Milwaukee

BEER STYLES

A GUIDE TO some of the major commercial beer styles, with three tasting terms to describe their characteristics.

Abbey (Ale)
Aromatic, full-flavoured, fruity.

Altbier (German Ale)
Malty, nutty, toasty.

American Pale Ale
Hop-dominant, citrus, pine.

Baltic Porter (most Porter is ale; this sub-style is Lager)
Liquorice, chocolate, dried fruit.

Barley Wine (Ale)
Malty, dried fruit, brandy.

Belgian Strong Dark Ale
Aromatic, caramel, fruity.

Belgian Strong Pale Ale
Aromatic, spicy, biscuity.

Berliner Weissbier (Ale and Mixed Fermentation)
Tart, lemon, sour.

Bière de Garde (usually Ale, but there are Lager versions)
Toasted, caramel, earthy.

Bitter (Ale)
Caramel, well-hopped, high bitterness.

Blonde Ale
Bready, lightly fruity, medium bitterness.

Bock (Lager)
Biscuity, toffee, fruity.

Brown Ale
Toffee, coffee, nutty.

Burton Ale
Fruity, malty, well-hopped.

Dortmunder Lager
Grassy, grainy, bready.

Extra Special Bitter (Ale)
Rich malt, toasty, fruity.

Flanders Red Ale (Mixed Fermentation)
Tangy, vinous, no bitterness.

Frambozen (Wild Fermentation but can also be Ale)
Sour raspberry, vanilla, tangy.

Golden Ale
Zesty, biscuity, fruity.

Gose (Ale and Mixed Fermentation)
Tart, gently salty, subtly fruity.

Gueuze (Wild Fermentation)
Earthy, dry, tart.

Hefeweizen *aka* Hefeweissbier, Weizen, Weisse, Wheat Beer (Ale)
Aromatic, spicy, tart.

Helles *aka* Hell (Lager)
Herbal, bready, light.

Imperial Russian Stout (Ale)
Roasted, coffee, liquorice.

India Pale Ale

There are so many iterations of IPA it is not possible to describe them in three phrases, but what they have in common is the dominance of hop flavours.

Kriek (Wild Fermentation but can also be Ale)

Sour cherry, vanilla, tangy.

Lambic (Wild Fermentation)

Sour, fruity, earthy.

Märzen *aka* Oktoberfestbier (Lager)

Bready, toasted caramel, low bitterness.

Mild (Ale)

Malty, caramel, low bitterness.

Old Ale

Dried fruit, caramel, malt.

Oud Bruin (Ale and Mixed Fermentation)

Spicy, dried fruit, sour.

Pale Ale

Biscuity, fruity, high bitterness.

Pilsner *aka* Pilsener (Lager)
Herbal, crisp, medium bitterness.

Porter (Ale)
Chocolate, coffee, savoury.

Rauchbier (can be Ale or Lager)
Smoky, malty, low bitterness.

Red Ale
Malty, fruity, medium bitterness.

Roggenbier (Rye Ale)
Malty bread, sour-sweet, spicy fruit.

Saison (Ale)
Spice, dry, earthy.

Schwarzbier (Lager)
Toasted malt, brown sugar, medium bitterness.

Scotch Ale
Caramel, dried fruit, malty.

Steam Beer *aka* California Common (Lager)
Biscuity, floral, lemon.

Stout (Ale)
There are many versions of this style, but dark stout is the
most widely brewed:
Charred, coffee, liquorice.

Trappist
Trappist is not a style per se, rather it is a legal term
that refers to the Trappist monks who brew a variety of
beers, including ones with full-flavoured, fruity, caramel
flavour profiles.

Vienna Lager
Caramel, bready, crisp.

Witbier (Ale)
Banana, cloves, tangy.

FURTHER READING

Stephen Harrod Buhner, *Sacred and Herbal Healing Beers* (Siris Books, 1998)

Rob DeSalle and Ian Tattersall, *A Natural History of Beer* (Yale University Press, 2019)

Patrick E. McGovern, *Uncorking the Past* (University of California Press, 2009)

Garret Oliver (Editor), *The Oxford Companion to Beer* (Oxford University Press, 2012)

Jane Peyton, *Beer O' Clock* (Summersdale, 2013)

Roger Protz, *IPA: A Legend in Our Time* (Pavilion, 2017)

LIST OF ILLUSTRATIONS

LIST OF ILLUSTRATIONS

Also available in this series

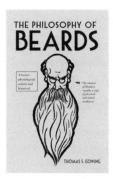